Getting to know you

You Are Worth Getting To Know

By

Isabel Contreras

ISBN: 1-4107-5065-5 (e-book)
ISBN: 1-4107-5064-7 (Paperback)

This book is printed on acid free paper.

Cover design by Isabel Contreras

1stBooks – rev. 08/15/03

This little book is dedicated to you. Enjoy it.

Acknowledgements

I am so grateful for the precious help of my beloved husband, Jakob Th. Möller, who had the patience to listen to me talk about my dreams; to my friends Sandra Cerutti, Kerrey d'Arcy, Miki Berge, Patricia Deane for their input, support and help with editing; and to my dear nephew/godson Christian Wyld, for drawing and creating the emotions. And above all thank you Nature for offering your inspiration. Just looking at you gave me an understanding of God's lavish abundance and a deeper understanding of myself and of life. All we need to know is laid out everywhere for us to see. We only need to focus, looking just a little closer to find it, to learn about the perfection of nature and to see, at the same time, the perfection of our own life. With "focus" by our side.

Thank you all for having contributed to the creation of this little book. With my deepest gratitude,

Isabel

Introduction

This was written in the middle of a quiet, silent and barren moment in my life, at a time when nothing was working for me, not even my health. And yet it allowed me to get to know all parts of myself: I started to explore the wonders of life and above all to learn never to give up.

This little book contains a dialogue with oneself about life's emotions, and in particular, a dialogue with Fear and Love. Fear explains why he exists at the emotional level, though he is not the fear we feel when in danger – which is a positive emotion – but rather the fear that stops us from moving on in our lives, the one that keeps us stuck. In this story "Spirit" is our other side, the one that is whole and pure – our true identity or, in other words, our real self (you know the one with a little voice that tells us when something is right or wrong – actually our intuitive part).

I speak about the emotions as either she or he. This is purely notional. The message came that way and it is a personal point of view.

Just imagine you are writing to your own self, or imagine sitting in front of a mirror and having a chat with yourself. At the end of the book you will have an opportunity to do so. Enjoy it.

PART I

Isabel Contreras

I have a wonderful friend close by my side. Sometimes he jumps on my right shoulder. His name is "Focus" and he is a tiny little felt monkey with so much personality. I have him in my workroom as a reminder to focus my attention on what I'm doing. He is so important

in keeping me from getting distracted. You see, we are like little monkeys, jumping from one side to the other, looking here, there and everywhere without knowing what we want, or afraid that we might be missing something very important.

In jumping about, we become scattered and unfocused – that is why my friend "Focus" has been with me for a long time. He has a very important job, to remind me to be CENTRED! When I learned to become CENTRED, I gradually got to know many parts of myself, becoming more conscious of my actions, my thoughts and my words. I knew deep down that these newly discovered parts of me had always been there, but as yet I did not know or understand why I had to learn about them.

One day, I went to Iceland to give a seminar on personal development. The place where the seminar was held is in the middle of nowhere. I stayed in a little cottage by myself, with no other people around. I was surrounded by nature, by the sea with its constant never-ending sound – a continuous cycle and recycle of the movement of the earth, influenced by the moon and the sun – by seagulls, lots of lava fields, a few empty summer houses, a majestic glacier, lots of fresh air and me.

I thought it would be good to spend a few days on my own before the seminar to prepare myself well and a few days again afterwards so that I could have some real time out – just me and nature.

I would like to mention that healthwise I was going through a very difficult time. Sometimes I thought I was not going to make it. It had lasted for more than two years. There was very little I could eat and my body was getting weaker and weaker. I put into practice all I was teaching and learning in order to help heal my body. But one thing I knew by intuition – I was going through this for a very specific reason, to learn something important! To have faith! Well, the challenge was there and I knew that out of this situation only good would come. Just as on a grey day we know that the sun is shining behind the cloud – we just cannot see it. But if we have faith and gratitude, we know that those grey and rainy days are also necessary in order to appreciate the sunshine more when it returns. I decided to treat my condition in the same way. Sounds easy when I talk about it, but at times it was not easy at all.

It was the beginning of a new experience. The next day when looking at myself in the mirror I said to myself 'Getting to know you' is what life is all about. I am willing to meet you – and this is what happened…I got to know my emotions very well. Being alone was magic for me, because it gave me the opportunity to get to know myself better without outside distractions.

Although my body was weak, my mind was getting stronger and stronger. I knew that in order to heal my body I needed to deal with my mind and understand my emotions. The following part will give you an opportunity to review how I imagined and experienced each of my emotions. It was as if they were really talking to me.

This dialogue was born in Brekkubaer, Iceland. I call that time my retreat period.

Isabel Contreras

PART II

Isabel Contreras

To the most beautiful person in the world

ME

Hello, I want to tell you how much I love you. This is something I recently discovered. And because of this new discovery, I have a burning desire to chat with you about our feelings. It has taken me so many years to actually understand them, so it is only now I can feel that I love you. I knew about loving oneself and I understood it intellectually, but I had not experienced feeling it one hundred percent. It is one thing to know with your mind and another to know with your inner self.

I felt there was something in me that needed to be fixed most of the time, or perhaps even always. I turned in circles trying to track down the famous "why". But in fact you (my spirit) loved me so much that you wanted me to learn about life. And for the same reason you made it difficult for me, even though things already seemed bad enough.

I knew that somewhere, deep inside me, a shining star was telling me that there was a lot more to learn, to feel, to understand – I just had to search. Then I discovered that things do not happen by accident, that they are meant to be, so that we can make progress and accept life more fully. This was when my inner journey began.

With this new realization that things do not happen by accident and that there is always a good reason behind everything that happens in our lives, I gained a new understanding that helped me to endure all my pains and difficulties in a gentler way, because I knew that out of each situation something good would ensue. So I began to get acquainted with a set of friends. Let me tell you more about them. At that time of my life, I got to know HOPE better. Indeed hope was so close to me that I started to feel safer and my life continued with lots of hope.

HAPPINESS was a real, true friend, because it had always been close to me. I felt happiness many times because I love life, people, nature and things in general. Happiness came easily to me.

I loved HAPPINESS.

But someone appeared along the way to disturb my friendship with HAPPINESS and HOPE: I met my greatest enemy, FEAR. When FEAR appeared unexpectedly, I became really, really blocked to the point that I forgot my best friend HAPPINESS. How long I had been fighting with my enemy I cannot tell. Not just for days

or months but for many years, maybe all my life. But then a miracle happened! You may find this hard to believe: FEAR became my friend.

Let me explain to you what actually happened…FEAR was very jealous of HAPPINESS because I always ignored Him. So FEAR tried so hard to be a pest that finally, lying on my bed to have a rest in my little bungalow, completely alone, my heart beating fast with FEAR inside, I said:

"OK FEAR, what do you want?"

and FEAR answered…looking at me with surprise…

"At last you are paying me some attention…I have good news for you and yet you have been ignoring me all this time. I have a mission to show you a magnificent shining star, and until you allow me to do so, I cannot leave you alone. If you only knew, I am actually your very best friend, because I have the key for you to open the most wonderful treasure you possess. This treasure is to discover who you really are. The real you, the wonderful star that you are and that shines permanently in your heart. By using this golden key you will find your treasure and see the magic that exists inside you. It has been such a long time and I have been working so hard to get your attention. I must say the Universe has given me the most difficult of all jobs. The Universe told me that only a strong and courageous emotion like me could be honoured with this job, because it requires a

11

certain amount of skill. So I want to share with you all the obstacles I had to go through to attract your attention and get you to take me seriously…Do you know anything about me? asked FEAR. I have feelings too!

When I came to you for the first time you rejected me. You did not want to know me because you were totally absorbed in the task of conquering HAPPINESS and you were afraid of me. But then my helpers came to give me a hand. They started to work on you and SHOCK took over.

This had an impact on you, because things were no longer going your way.

Then SORROW followed to teach you more about JOY. This

was a very hard discovery, but eventually you started to learn that JOY is even greater than HAPPINESS.

Next LONELINESS appeared and you really felt its presence. At that moment, you realised that you were alone with your emotions. HAPPINESS was always your goal but had moved

Insecurity

beyond reach because INSECURITY had become like a parasite – so difficult to get rid of. He actually liked you.

ANGER did not like INSECURITY

because it gave you a feeling of low self-esteem. So ANGER came and set about clearing up the mess. He comes

from time to time to prevent RESENTMENT from taking over and getting you into the habit of blaming others and/or events for what has gone wrong. When this happens, guess who your next friend is?

Here comes SELF-PITY. She really knows how to make friends with you. But eventually you became tired of SELF-PITY, with her lack of creativity and her draining effect. You called on your old friend HOPE again, and that was the

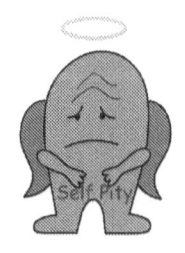

moment when a new friend arrived on his White Horse,

brandishing the sword of victory and declaring: "I have arrived! My name is DOUBT and I have come to show you what my talents are, so you can learn to choose and make decisions."

FEAR continues…

"As you can see, I had a lot of trouble with DOUBT as it overshadowed me. And so, fearfully skilled with my straightforward line, I had to help you deal with DOUBT, because it was interfering, confusing you and giving you so many alternatives that it made you forget your goal, remember?"

"Yes, HAPPINESS."

FEAR continues…

"Again you became afraid of me because you felt fear. However, it did not last. After a while you became sick and tired of DOUBT telling you all the time, "when in DOUBT, there is a choice". You didn't know what to do any more and clarity was lost. You had so many desires and could hardly fulfil any of them. You were so busy with all my co-workers. So DESIRE became a solid friend, one far more creative than HOPE, and you both built castles in the air – much to the joy of ILLUSION. This was fun even though I FEAR, still weighed heavily on you. But then you became aware of ILLUSION.

Amazingly, you gradually understood that in fact ILLUSION does not exist at all except in your mind.

You eventually reached the point where you couldn't take it any more and stood up to face me."

"All right FEAR!

Enough is enough! You have won! Now tell me, what do you want?"

FEAR continues…

"I turned towards you and humbly said: Look me straight in the eyes. The time has come for you to know that behind each FEAR hides a shining Star. This is what I wanted so much to reveal to you. Look behind your fear to see it closely, feel it and discover the shining Star in your heart. This Star symbolises new beginnings and guidance. So you see my role has been to help you discover who I am – a way to look at life differently."

Then I asked FEAR:

"Can you show me the way and maybe we can be friends?"

And FEAR showed me the way by giving me a golden key to find and open my treasure.

Living with FEAR was not always easy, as sometimes I experienced emotional pain and physical discomfort. I was not used to facing FEAR and at times became afraid. Deep down, though, I knew I was never alone because a little voice whispered in my ear: *"Remember what you once learned? Feel the fear and do it anyway."* This gave me the strength to look closely at FEAR again, and guess what? I discovered the beginning of a new Life.

By looking inside FEAR I found the treasure I was looking for, and when I opened it with the golden key I went into the Future and found the real ME, a shining star: talented, beautiful, loving, caring, joyful, intelligent, agile, capable, adventurous, creative, fearless, courageous, an excellent communicator, friendly, compassionate, funny, happy, curious, prosperous, joyous, looking forward to learning and experiencing new things. In short, a beautiful human being with a heart of gold and a shining star in the middle.

Suddenly I felt a gentle presence and a beautiful friend appeared saying:

"Hello, my name is LOVE and I have come here to be with you forever. You know that wherever you go, I go, and whatever you do, I do. We are inseparable and together we shall succeed. I wish you every success with me by your side and I know you are always safe when you are with me. Always remember to ask yourself when resting 'Who are you?' and wait for the answer, and then 'What do you want?' and again wait for the answer. Do this several times running.'

In times of turmoil, doubt and fear, add FAITH and TRUST through gratitude. Practice gratitude as much as you can. Remember that too much is never too much when you are grateful. This will connect you back to me. I love you."

"Thank you LOVE, I have a question for you. How can I learn to have faith and trust so that I can get to know you better? I have learnt many things, but these I do not yet know very well."

"Perfect question", answers LOVE. *"Quite, we don't learn much about them, do we? If I recall, you are only <u>told</u> to love, to have faith, to trust, to do this, to do that, and so on. Often, you are not actually <u>taught</u> how. To learn about faith and trust requires a very simple skill, practising gratitude!…And looking at FEAR in the eye.*

When you fall in love, no one has ever told you to practise falling in love. You just do and you just know and you automatically have faith in your feelings and simply trust. And you are so grateful. Then, with time, you may start to get hurt and disappointed. You forget to trust and faith is eliminated from your being. You forget what love really was for you. You only remember the pain, the hurt, the disappointment. You close the door to love, faith and trust. The good news is that,

having experienced love, you possess the ability to love, like everyone else on this planet."

Again I asked LOVE:

"How can I learn about true love, with trust and faith by my side?"

LOVE replied…

"Again, practise GRATITUDE. Gratitude in every aspect of your life. Always remember that faith is born of gratitude, followed by me. Look into your eyes in the mirror; put your hands on the area of your heart and say (if possible aloud and with compassion): I love you and I want to know you. Repeat the following:"

YES, I am…

Immune to criticism
Beneath and above no one
Fearless
I respect you
I encourage you
I support you
I love you

ALWAYS

YES, I am

my best friend!

LOVE continues…

"This is so powerful that within a short period of time you will start experiencing the miraculous feelings of my presence: LOVE, followed by TRUST and FAITH in every aspect of your life. You will simply know what is best for you.

Remember that repetition of positive statements with a visual picture in your mind, mixed with happy thoughts and lots of GRATITUDE, create positive results. You truly are what you think about. Practise this, it cannot fail. It can only improve the quality of your life.

You may have worked out that I am very easy to learn. I only require practice, gratitude and willingness. Try practising becoming a child, being playful and spontaneous, and you will experience being yourself and experience the wonderful feeling of LOVE and CONFIDENCE.

One more important thing I would like you to know. Allow me to introduce you to COURAGE as he has a very important message for you.

Hello, COURAGE is my name and it is a pleasure to be with you, helped by my co-worker and friend STRENGTH. Together, we work hand in hand and you will be surprised to learn that we have a  *direct link to the Universe. Our fuel/energy is the sun. When you are with us you succeed because you develop a strong action capacity. Even if you feel that you have failed, always remember that*  *failure isn't fatal and that success isn't forever, as there is everlasting change and that there are other ways forward. As you develop more COURAGE, you become stronger and stronger, eventually earning the medal of COURAGE to take action. Action is in direct contact with the sun's energy. Think about that.*

Walking alongside LOVE and CONFIDENCE, you will get to know us and become part of the universal harmony that exists within us all.

With this realization you will immediately become acquainted and at ease with your other friends who are waiting to be united with you, offering their services because they are creative – which is your true

essence. So let me introduce you to TALENT, FUN and HUMOUR. They are truly magic. They work together on a permanent basis and through their work produce absolute

JOY. When JOY is in your life you are always satisfied and fulfilled.

When TALENT reaches your spirit, you are suffused with

something wonderful. Suddenly you do the things you love without effort, with FUN, LAUGHTER and good HUMOUR as staunch friends. Doing and being inspirational with JOY by your side. It is absolute bliss."

LOVE continues…

"Open your heart to learn new things and start living your life with LOVE and CONFIDENCE, developing friendship with COURAGE, STRENGTH, TALENT, FUN, JOY and WISDOM by your side as your friends. WISDOM is the real you that knows what is best for you and you feel content with who you are"

"Thank you LOVE. I am happy to have you by my side."

"So what do you think?" I asked myself, and I answered myself:

"Not bad – after all, it really is excellent. I am so proud that you have had the courage to meet FEAR and all his co-workers and have got to know them. Even better, LOVE, which is a permanent and everlasting emotion and is genuinely awesome."

Well, you know…I began to believe that all these friends, called emotions, awareness and feelings, are actually real. So

FEAR, HOPE, DESIRE, ANGER, RESENTMENT, INSECURITY, SELF-PITY, DOUBT, LONELINESS, SORROW AND ILLUSION, have been good to us. They have all been our teachers. They have all taught us a little bit of what their mission is, and if they come again I know they come to teach me more of who I am. Because all these friends, called emotions, awareness and feelings, are what make us special and unique. They are actually part of me, you and everyone in the world.

Do you know that getting to know them for what they are will open the door to meeting our other friends? You know, those that we so often pray to have in our life? Yes...LOVE, CONFIDENCE, COURAGE, HAPPINESS, TALENT, HUMOUR, GRATITUDE, STRENGTH, FUN, LAUGHTER, JOY and WISDOM and all the great positive experiences, awareness, feelings and emotions LOVE talked about.

So, one very important thing I have learned: if the old and new friends come again, I promise that I will look them straight in the eye and never ignore them ever again. Because they are our advisers, our friends and our teachers, who help us become the person that we were born to be, with LOVE by our side.

By the way, have you noticed that they come and go? That is why they have wings; they fly in and fly out depending on the situation in life. They are always hanging in there ready for action. Never under estimate them, they have a function.

Well, I guess that's it for now. It was nice chatting with you for the first time. I will write to you often so that we can be up to date with the latest news of the new us. Now I know that life is full of opportunities and choices to make and I will continue with GRATITUDE, FAITH, TRUST, COURAGE, STRENGTH, HUMOUR, LOVE, CONFIDENCE and WISDOM by my side.

I love you, my own best friend: **ME.**

PS. You are worth getting to know!

(The following pages are specially designed for you to keep a journal and write to yourself as often as you wish – something special or just a dialogue about how you feel and what you want – and to practice using your intuition by just writing what comes to mind. This will give you the opportunity to go over your journal from time to time to see how you have been progressing in your life. What you thought and felt one time may be so different the next time you write to yourself. It is a wonderful way to keep a personal dialogue with yourself and, above all, to keep track of personal progress over a period of 12 months. In my life, I practice this on a daily basis and I call it my morning discoveries. First thing in the morning when I open my eyes I write what comes to mind. It is a wonderful way to offer your brain some gymnastics and believe me, your brain will be good to you in return, effective, clear, innovative, creative, inspirational and above all, a very useful tool to have.)

Isabel Contreras

My journal

Date_____

Isabel Contreras

Dear Me,

_____

_____

_____

_____

_____

_____

_____

_____

_____

_____

_____

_____

_____

_____

_____

_____

_____

_____

_____

_____

_____

_____

Isabel Contreras

_____
_____
_____
_____
_____
_____
_____
_____
_____
_____
_____
_____
_____
_____
_____
_____
_____

My new commitment:_____
_____
_____
_____
_____
_____
_____
_____

Sign:_____Date:___ _____

Dear Me,

_____

_____

_____

_____

_____

_____

_____

_____

_____

_____

_____

_____

_____

_____

_____

_____

_____

_____

_____

_____

_____

_____

Isabel Contreras

_____

_____

_____

_____

_____

_____

_____

_____

_____

_____

_____

_____

_____

_____

_____

_____

_____

_____

My new commitment:_____

_____

_____

_____

_____

_____

Sign:_____Date: _____

Dear Me,

_____

_____

_____

_____

_____

_____

_____

_____

_____

_____

_____

_____

_____

_____

_____

_____

_____

_____

_____

_____

_____

_____

_____

_____

_____

_____

_____

_____

_____

_____

_____

_____

_____

_____

_____

_____

_____

_____

_____

_____

_____

My new commitment:_____

_____

_____

_____

_____

_____

_____

Sign:_____Date:_____

Dear Me,

_____

_____

_____

_____

_____

_____

_____

_____

_____

_____

_____

_____

_____

_____

_____

_____

_____

_____

_____

_____

_____

_____

_____

Isabel Contreras

_____

_____

_____

_____

_____

_____

_____

_____

_____

_____

_____

_____

_____

_____

_____

_____

_____

_____

My new commitment:_____

_____

_____

_____

_____

Sign:_____Date: _____

Dear Me,

_____

_____

_____

_____

_____

_____

_____

_____

_____

_____

_____

_____

_____

_____

_____

_____

_____

_____

_____

_____

_____

_____

_____

_____

Isabel Contreras

_____

_____

_____

_____

_____

_____

_____

_____

_____

_____

_____

_____

_____

_____

_____

My new commitment:_____

_____

_____

_____

_____

_____

Sign:_____Date:___ _____

Dear Me,

_____

_____

_____

_____

_____

_____

_____

_____

_____

_____

_____

_____

_____

_____

_____

_____

_____

_____

_____

_____

_____

_____

_____

Isabel Contreras

_____

_____

_____

_____

_____

_____

_____

_____

_____

_____

_____

_____

_____

_____

_____

_____

_____

My new commitment:_____

_____

_____

_____

_____

_____

Sign:_____Date: _____

Dear Me,

_____

_____

_____

_____

_____

_____

_____

_____

_____

_____

_____

_____

_____

_____

_____

_____

_____

_____

_____

_____

_____

_____

_____

Isabel Contreras

_____

_____

_____

_____

_____

_____

_____

_____

_____

_____

_____

_____

_____

_____

_____

My new commitment:_____

_____

_____

_____

_____

_____

_____

Sign:_____Date:___ _____

Dear Me,

_____

_____

_____

_____

_____

_____

_____

_____

_____

_____

_____

_____

_____

_____

_____

_____

_____

_____

_____

_____

_____

_____

_____

_____

Isabel Contreras

_____

_____

_____

_____

_____

_____

_____

_____

_____

_____

_____

_____

_____

_____

_____

_____

_____

My new commitment:_____

_____

_____

_____

_____

Sign:_____Date: _____

Dear Me,

_____

_____

_____

_____

_____

_____

_____

_____

_____

_____

_____

_____

_____

_____

_____

_____

_____

_____

_____

_____

_____

_____

_____

Isabel Contreras

_____

_____

_____

_____

_____

_____

_____

_____

_____

_____

_____

_____

_____

_____

_____

My new commitment:_____

_____

_____

_____

_____

_____

Sign:_____Date:___ _____

Dear Me,

_____

_____

_____

_____

_____

_____

_____

_____

_____

_____

_____

_____

_____

_____

_____

_____

_____

_____

_____

_____

_____

_____

Isabel Contreras

_____

_____

_____

_____

_____

_____

_____

_____

_____

_____

_____

_____

_____

_____

_____

_____

_____

_____

My new commitment:_____

_____

_____

_____

_____

Sign:_____Date: _____

Dear Me,

_____

_____

_____

_____

_____

_____

_____

_____

_____

_____

_____

_____

_____

_____

_____

_____

_____

_____

_____

_____

_____

_____

_____

_____

Isabel Contreras

_____

_____

_____

_____

_____

_____

_____

_____

_____

_____

_____

_____

_____

_____

_____

_____

My new commitment:_____

_____

_____

_____

_____

_____

Sign:_____Date:___ _____

Dear Me,

_____

_____

_____

_____

_____

_____

_____

_____

_____

_____

_____

_____

_____

_____

_____

_____

_____

_____

_____

_____

_____

_____

Isabel Contreras

_____

_____

_____

_____

_____

_____

_____

_____

_____

_____

_____

_____

_____

_____

_____

My new commitment:_____

_____

_____

_____

_____

_____

Sign:_____Date: _____

About the Author

 ISABEL CONTRERAS' journey has taken her to experience life in different ways. With the ups and downs that life offers she took the path of least resistance to find herself and the meaning of life. She took extensive training to understand why we are the way we are so as to discover the gift of life. She is now committed to assisting others find their life's journey. She holds a diploma in Positive Thinking Counselling, she is a certified self-development teacher and coach, NLP practitioner and a Transformational Breathing facilitator. In addition to her individualized private practice as a counsellor coach and therapist, she is the founder of Life Motivations, a Center for life management skills and wellbeing in Switzerland and conducts seminars, training courses and workshops in English and French.

Life Motivations

Centre for Life Management Skills and Wellbeing

5 Chemin de la Radio

Colovrex

1293 Bellevue (Switzerland)

www.lifemotivations.ch

lifemotivations@aol.com